First Facts®

The Middle Ages

The Miserable Life of Medieval Peasants

by Jim Whiting

Consultant:
James Masschaele
Associate Professor of Medieval History
Rutgers University
New Brunswick, New Jersey

Capstone
press®

Mankato, Minnesota

First Facts is published by Capstone Press,
151 Good Counsel Drive, P.O. Box 669, Mankato, Minnesota 56002.
www.capstonepress.com

♻ Books published by Capstone Press are manufactured with paper
containing at least 10 percent post-consumer waste.

Library of Congress Cataloging-in-Publication Data
Whiting, Jim, 1943–
    The miserable life of medieval peasants / by Jim Whiting.
    p. cm. — (First facts. The Middle Ages)
    Summary: "Describes the lives of medieval peasants, including their jobs, homes, and
daily life" — Provided by publisher.
    Includes bibliographical references and index.
    ISBN 978-1-4296-3335-2 (library binding)
    1. Peasantry — Europe — History — Juvenile literature. 2. Europe — Social conditions
— To 1492 — Juvenile literature. 3. Europe — Social life and customs — Juvenile literature.
4. Social history — Medieval, 500–1500 — Juvenile literature. I. Title. II. Series.
HD1523.W457 2010
305.5′6330940902 — dc22   2009005059

Editorial Credits
Megan Schoeneberger, editor; Kim Brown, set designer; Matt Bruning, book designer;
    Svetlana Zhurkin, media researcher

Photo Credits
Alamy/Interfoto Pressebildagentur, cover; Alamy/The London Art Archive, 15; Alamy/
Peter Barritt, 16–17; Art Resource, N.Y./Giraudon, 9 (right); Art Resource, N.Y./Scala, 4–5;
British Library, London, UK/British Library Board. All Rights Reserved/The Bridgeman
Art Library, 8–9; Getty Images/The Bridgeman Art Library, 1, 7, 18; Getty Images/Hulton
Archive, 6; Glasgow University Library, Scotland/The Bridgeman Art Library, 10; Mary
Evans Picture Library, 20; Musee Conde, Chantilly, France/The Bridgeman Art Library, 12
(left); North Wind Picture Archives, 12–13

Essential content terms are **bold** and are defined at the bottom of the page where they
first appear.

Table of Contents

Not Such a Good Life

In the Middle Ages, **peasants** lived hard lives. They began work at dawn and fell into bed soon after sunset. They ate crummy food. They hardly ever changed their clothes. Their small houses smelled awful.

∾∾∾∾∾∾∾∾∾∾∾∾∾∾∾∾∾∾∾∾∾∾∾∾∾

peasant — a poor farmer

4

Peasants in the
Middle Ages
Europe
476 – 1500

5

Hard at Work

Peasant men worked long hours in the fields. They plowed fields and planted seeds. They also pulled weeds and harvested crops by hand.

Peasant women worked just as hard. They were in charge of household chores. They cleaned and cooked while caring for their children.

Medieval Fact

Peasant families didn't bathe very often. So they smelled pretty bad. When they did take baths, everyone used the same bathwater.

Home Small Home

Peasants' houses often had just one room. A cooking fire gave off the only heat and light. Smoke curled out through a hole in the **thatched** roof.

Peasants did not have much furniture. Everyone slept on straw mattresses laid on the dirt floor. They used logs as pillows.

thatched — made of straw

Lots of Company

Peasants often brought their cattle, sheep, and chickens inside at night. Other critters also lived with peasants. Birds, mice, and insects made nests in the thatched roofs.

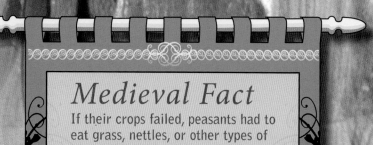

Mealtime

Peasants didn't have very much food. They sometimes went hungry. They grew vegetables in small gardens. They gathered nuts and berries in nearby forests. Lucky ones had a few scraps of meat. Dinner was usually **pottage** and bread. Water was often dirty and loaded with germs. Everyone drank beer or **ale**.

pottage — a thick stew made of vegetables, grain, and sometimes meat

ale — a drink similar to beer

Fast Food in the Middle Ages

Armies in the Middle Ages usually didn't carry food with them. But the soldiers still needed to eat. They took food from peasants whose lands they crossed. If the peasants complained, they were sometimes killed.

What Peasants Wore

Peasants wore the same clothing for weeks at a time. Men had shirts and short pants. Women wore long dresses. Nearly everything was made of scratchy wool.

Kid Stuff

Daily life was grim, but kids still had fun. They played with spinning tops, dolls, and other toys. They pretended that pieces of wood were knights and soldiers. They played hide-and-seek. In winter they went ice-skating and had snowball fights.

Medieval Fact

Playtime ended when children were about 7 years old. Boys went to work in the fields. Girls helped around the house. Very few children went to school.

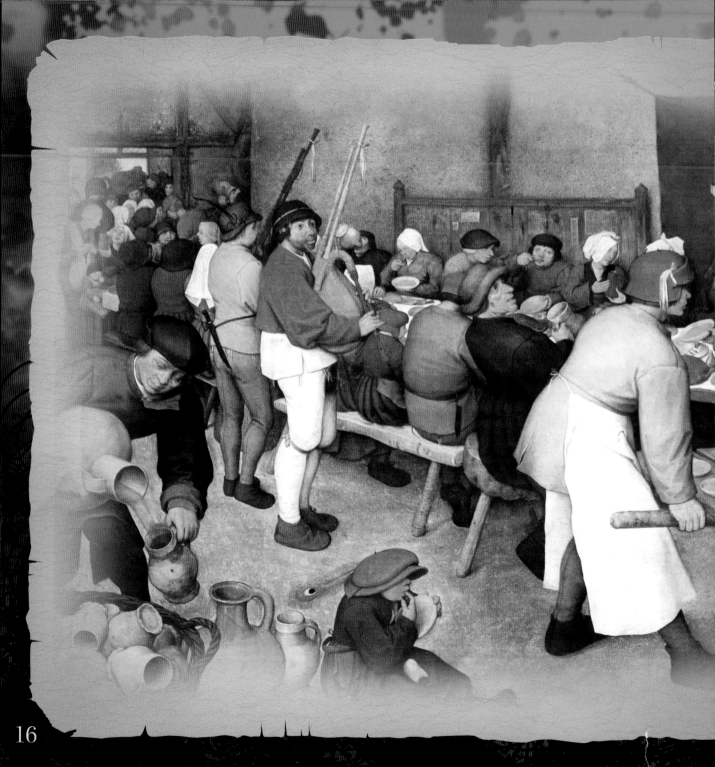

Taking a Break

Adults also had some breaks in their hard lives. On Sundays they went to church. They enjoyed feasts on church holy days. They danced and played games. They also celebrated marriages and births.

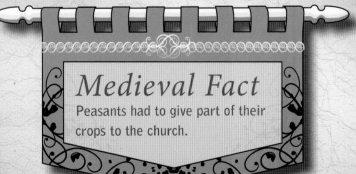

Medieval Fact

Peasants had to give part of their crops to the church.

Medieval Fact

Most peasants spent their whole lives within a few miles of where they were born.

Changing Times

A **plague** called the Black Death swept through Europe around 1350. Millions of peasants died. But life got better for the ones who lived. After the plague, there was a shortage of workers. Many peasants moved to towns. They got better jobs. In time, the Middle Ages ended.

plague — a disease that spreads quickly and kills many people

Amazing but True!

Life for left-handed peasants was especially miserable in the Middle Ages. Most people believed the devil was left-handed. So left-handers were thought of as servants of the devil. They were accused of having evil powers.

Try It Out:
Play Hunt the Slipper

Peasant children in the Middle Ages liked to play Hunt the Slipper. You and your friends can travel back in time by playing the same game.

What You Need

a group of five or more friends
a shoe or slipper

What You Do

1. Choose one person to be the Slipper Soul. Everyone else is a Cobbler, a person who makes or repairs shoes.
2. The Cobblers stand in a line facing the Slipper Soul.
3. The Slipper Soul hands the slipper to a Cobbler. The Slipper Soul then closes his or her eyes and chants, "Cobbler! Cobbler! Mend my shoe! Fix it up and make it new! One, two, three, four stitches will do!"
4. During the chant, the Cobblers pass the shoe around, keeping it hidden behind their backs. After the chant, the Slipper Soul opens his or her eyes and tries to guess which Cobbler has the slipper. If the Slipper Soul is right, the Cobbler with the slipper changes places with the Slipper Soul. If not, the Slipper Soul takes another turn.

Glossary

ale (AYL) — a drink similar to beer

peasant (PEZ-uhnt) — a poor farmer

plague (PLAYG) — a very serious disease that spreads quickly to many people and often causes death

pottage (POT-ij) — a stew made by boiling vegetables, grain, and sometimes meat

thatched (THACHD) — made of straw

Read More

Hull, Robert. *Peasant.* Smart Apple Media Medieval Lives. Mankato, Minn.: Black Rabbit Books, 2009.

Johnson, Sheri. *Kids in the Medieval World.* The Middle Ages. Mankato, Minn.: Capstone Press, 2009.

Shuter, Jane. *The Middle Ages.* History Opens Windows. Chicago: Heinemann, 2007.

Internet Sites

FactHound offers a safe, fun way to find Internet sites related to this book. All of the sites on FactHound have been researched by our staff.

Here's all you do:

Visit *www.facthound.com*

FactHound will fetch the best sites for you!

Index